Shaken Down

'The art of our necessities is strange,
And can make vile things precious.'

King Lear, Act III Sc. ii.

Ki te hunga mate me te hunga ora nō Ōtautahi:
To the dead and living of Christchurch

SHAKEN DOWN 6.3

*Poems from the second Christchurch
earthquake, 22 February 2011*

Jeffrey Paparoa Holman

ꟻ𝒥ℴℎ𝓂𝓃

ᴜᴩ

Canterbury University Press

UC

UNIVERSITY OF
CANTERBURY
Te Whare Wānanga o Waitaha
CHRISTCHURCH NEW ZEALAND

First published in 2012 by
CANTERBURY UNIVERSITY PRESS
University of Canterbury
Private Bag 4800, Christchurch
NEW ZEALAND
www.cup.canterbury.ac.nz

ISBN 978-1-927145-30-2

A catalogue record for this book is available from the
National Library of New Zealand

Pre-production courtesy of Steele Roberts Publishers, Wellington
Printed by PrintStop, Wellington

The poems in this collection were written while the author was the 2011
writer in residence at the University of Waikato, with support from
Creative New Zealand, to whom acknowledgment is due.

ARTS COUNCIL OF NEW ZEALAND TOI AOTEAROA

The following poems have been previously published: 'September 'quake':
Press, Christchurch; 'Who of you': Landfall 222; 'The several joys of
an earthquake': New Zealand Listener; 'After the tremor': New Zealand
Booksellers online, www.booksellers.co.nz.

Contents

September 'quake

Our chimneys came to life
bricks became birds
flew through roofs onto cars
landing on lawns building up terror

Night with a crack made its move
tiles turned to leaves and fell
lay on the lawns
in terracotta glory

The roads were rivers
rubble the shops
theatrefronts fell
foundations were flowing

Neighbour is clasping
next-door neighbour
strangers are standing
strangers no longer

History houses hopes clattered down
fear came thundering love stood its ground

Two days later the cat comes back
two days later she pads on in
two days gone she licks her paws
two days later she's purring again

the several joys of an earthquake

to have the egg of my ego
smashed
to feel the couch of comfort
buckle
to know the world's not at
my feet
to find my upside upside
down
to know there are real lives
next door
to cower when the elements
roar
to have the umbilical sac
of materiality

answered back

civilisation

I turn on the tap and water flows.
I lay on paste and clean my teeth.
I pee in the bowl and flush it.

I turn on the light and the power is there.
The radio too and I'm not alone.
The TV flares and the world appears.

The ground seems still beneath my feet.
Sailor ashore I can feel the sea
even when I know it isn't

moving
        rolling
making
        waves.

us

the train rolls past
and I lie here
beneath Waikato stars
dreaming a dream
of one of them

Te Taki Tairakena

the train has gone
I dream on
the stars are where
they always are
wordlessly observing
us

Te Taki Tainamaiti Tairakena (Wally), teacher of English.
Died in the CTV building collapse, 22 February 2011.

who of you

who of you
will not now bow
pay homage to
Unbrick & Unstone?

See how they unlay unstack undo
all we have ever done.

Who can stand against them
when they come
with their earth whips their land hooks?

They have toppled cross
from steeple
they have murdered
people.

Unbrick Unstone
unlay unstack undo
turn smashed every human
clock back.

after the tremor

after the tremor the neighbour
after the terror the stranger
after the stranger the doctor
after the doctor the soldier
after the soldier the looter
after the looter the vulture

after the horror the ruins
after the ruins the kindness
after the kindness the sirens
after the sirens the silence
after the silence the weeping
after the weeping the comfort

after the toppling the creaking
after the shaking the shaking
after the shaking the questions
after the questions the questions
after the rage and courage
after profound desolation

after the nurse and the undertaker
we stand and we drink from a glass of water

when all you

when all you
ever hoped and made

is scattered and laid

here there and every possible where
in this room and that   on that street and lawn
when intimate details flutter down from
seven storeys high
you don't know where mother brother lover sister

or dog

are &
the world is shattered and laid to rest
creaks and hisses beneath an impossible weight

the heart pumps
and flutters like so many trapped birds

when this is it   when the lines do not begin and end like a real poem
a proper poem   a gracious ordered sinuous well-behaved poem

& you stagger to stand on the deck of the earth   you're a sailor now

on the storm

of the world.

this fly: earthquake

this fly
he circles and circles
me

it's not just another human
disaster to him

in the compound world-view
of a fly's eye

it's a business
opportunity

tall buildings

Yesterday we were tall buildings.
Today we are falling leaves.
Autumn, and the bricks are turning

bronze, golden yellow, paper
pale, they are laid beside us in
evening grasses. Yesterday we

were those with stories. Today,
every breath is a breath away.

Tauwhare Marae

Sendai: mō te hunga mate, 22.2.2011–11.3.2011.

Anywhere: stand on this broken
sphere, you are never far
from victims.

Wherever: there you are with them
at the opposite pole, where the whirlpool
bends.

Forever near and bound by
blood now: ancient, Japanese,
Māori.

On furthest ends of the armour
plate — the same sudden
fate.

When his karanga came to call, you
died there with him and live
here now.

Everywhere's here in the world's dark
room: in the underworld, in
the urupā.

poor bare forked animal

(King Lear, *Act III Sc.iv*)

take physic pomp
(no fault of mine)

tak fizzik pompous
(the earth is thinking)

fizzing cracking smashing Pompeii
(underneath a train is rumbling)

tak a tak smack a smack pom pom pom
(the world the world the world's a beast)

take my hand it's terror in paradise
(hold me see my heart's a-chattering)

tak phyzhik pomp thou art exposed
(the moor is heaving all's at sea)

tak fizzik thou poor fork-ed beast
(the moon and sun at war with me)

fizzik Pompey's good for thee
(I know I know the wretch I am)

poor bare broken thing
(my Lear my Fool my kingdom down)

memory is place

memory is
the braille of buildings
threading the labyrinth

how can I find
my way through myself
with the past torn down

the road of dreams
with my compass
smashed

memory is the street
where love
struck

avenues where lips
came close to giving
desire a name

writing letters
on every brick
knowing

we could always come
and find the places
kisses met

Mother Earth speaks on desire and rue

my hand was on the city
I let go
my heart was on desire
till I met rue

my heart was with my lover
now I know
cathedrals have no answer
to you

my longing tugged at autumn
in the mist
my world collapsed before
the leaves turned pale

the gate is swinging open
and the door
the thoroughfare is silent
and the birds

when earth my mother finally came
to call
she shook me by the scruff
and asked me — 'Well?'

my heart was in a country
disappeared
desire that turned to rue
will lead me back

sleep is the balm

sleep is the balm
where forgetting happens
but we can't forget

with incense burning nightly
for the dead

when all the sticks are broken
and dreams are dreams of roads
where no one goes

you rise and nothing seems the same
what was is not
what is

to sleep now is to wake
in streets that won't
stop shaking

against condescension

learn to love your grandmother's songs
show some respect
poems her brothers took to war
humble lines that helped them die

he faced a kamikaze
a copy of Kipling's *If* in his wallet
see what that sneer
has done to your lips

think of yourself in a fallen building
ticking away in darkness
The Lord is my shepherd
I shall not want

culture my culture composed
me a songbook: *Twilight Time*
Red Sails in the Sunset
Nearer, my God, to Thee

when we were boys we had all the answers
when we were girls we knew it all
the dead were dumb in another room
behind a condescending wall

Kashii Beach tangi: for Ken

A wooden bench, a poem on stone: sakura blossom
pink and tender floods the park with a sea of petals.

Ah, the Manyoshu Tanka Monument!
I come upon you after all these years,
a stranger: so many blossoms
fell in Tōhoku! Even in my faraway
country, people cried for you.

And these are your oldest poems, the steel
sign tells me: 'Everyone, let us gather seaweed
for our breakfast, wetting the sleeves
of our white robes.' The scenery at Kashii
Beach that once could be seen from this hill
has also provoked to verse on the sign
an official of the Fukuoka Board of Education.

'From tomorrow,' the Manyoshu poet
inscribes, 'I will have no chance of seeing
the Kashii Beach again, which I have
always seen as I came and went.'

I photograph the petalled sea: *fubuki, fubuki.*
I feel these fallen flyers strike my heart.

Kashii, Kyushu, Japan: 15 April 2011.

Manyoshu	6th century.
Sakura	Cherry blossom. Symbol of beauty, transience and the kamikaze pilots.
Tanka	Poetical form.
Fubuki	The time when the flowering cherry blossoms fly in the winds and fall.
Tōhoku	Northeastern Honshu, where the Sendai earthquake and tsunami struck.

Miyagi prefecture: 11 March 2011

everyone knows
one Japanese word:
tsunami

cars: toys
houses: toys
ships: toys

you on the bridge
watching the warehouse
sailing by — run!

awe struck
jaw drops
mesmerised

the paralysed
the panicked of NHK studios
live news

praying crying
everywhere
in waves about to die

Densinya rice haiku

egret waits
white spear
by green rice blades

    happy frog
    by rice blades
    hears the oxen come

        foolish oxen-hearing
        frog forgets
        the egret's knife

egret swallows
kicking legs
and night has come

    under the moon
    the paddy shivers
    one frog less

        thousands taken
        at Tōhoku: no one
        to eat rice

recovery positions

keep it in the now for now
don't dwell on the former dwellings

we'll build where the old
buildings were

as long as we're alive we're here
keep it in the now for now

keep it in the moment's the way
don't waste your tears
on yesterday or tomorrow

that shop that fence that place that corner
you still remember
that tree that roof that ridgeline on the hill
the one-time neighbour
cafés theatres boulevards of the mind
leave behind

for now

living with heroes

I was living with heroes
and blind at the time

heroes who daily faced death from the sky
damp nights passed in their holes underground
as the ordnance of darkness came toppling down
counting the breaths of the blasting about them
cuddling the terrier choking back terror

I ate with survivors
unwitting of this

survivors of streets that became in the night
junkyards of grief and mortuary rows
abbatoirs where the blood would bloom
in gardens where the roses were
the dust of hell was everywhere
as in the detail devils shrieked

I slept with survivors
deaf to their dreams

dreams where the earth was nowhere to be seen
caves where the sirens would wail like mothers
keening on mountains for every lost human
dreams where fathers ground teeth in their sleeping
nightmares where even the nightmare was weeping

I'm living with heroes
a life upside down

the city a brickyard
the streets rollercoasters
attacks from below that we cannot prepare for
we turn to each other and open our eyes
we feel that the earth has come into our hearts
we're shaken together

at last

bearing up

slim single volumes of poetry
populate the designated areas
of their subject on library shelves
they are there, but not to be found

when they first appear they are few
in number and failing to make a splash
are soon forgotten, some say because
no one is listening, others say the moon

has cursed them, cursed them for saying
too much at the wrong time, left them out
in the cold, never there at natural
disasters in sufficient numbers

content to talk to each other and not the dead
the dead who can tell them what to say
to the living: how to meet every human need
and still sing, still bear weight, still be made

of blood and bone, carry the words of the world
to lighten the living, to lift their load

alone

I am alone
I am not on my own
outside the window, birds, traffic

you are alone
you are not on your own
through the ether, voices, static

we are alone
we are not on our own
down the ages call the ancients

no one alone
none on their own
waiting after death

the lovers

Miner, by Steve Newby

About suffering: can art help us to bear life's blows?

*There are knocks in life so hard, I don't know
knocks like God's hatred
César Vallejo, 1892–1938*[1]

I WROTE THE POEMS in this series for my own sake and
sanity, at a time when my world and that of everyone
in Christchurch had been shaken up and turned —
in an emotional and spiritual sense as well — upside
down. If they speak to anyone else, that is a bonus; for
me, it was a way of taking ownership and some kind
of control over an inner world that was manifesting
the outward chaos. Inwardly, it was exhausting, and I
was one of the lucky ones: minimal property damage,
and then a year away up north on a writing residency
at the University of Waikato beckoning.

Even so, I was home in bed on the night of 4
September 2010, and resident in Christchurch through
until early January, in the aftermath of aftershocks. I
was home for a break on 17 February, just in time for
the killer earthquake on the 22nd. I was back again in
June for the two shakes on the 13th — so far, I seem
to have managed to be around when the major shocks
hit. I think I can speak about fear and sleeplessness,
adrenalin shocks and post-traumatic stress disorder,
about what it feels like to sense you have lost control
of your life — and the grief that comes when a close
and dear friend dies in a building collapse. These forces,
natural and geological, human and metaphysical, were
what provoked the poems.

Many of them surfaced in the early hours of the
morning in Hamilton as I lay awake listening to the

49

trains rumbling through Frankton, once more unable to get an unbroken night's sleep. I got used to getting up and writing, then working on whatever came through. It became clear to me that this was a necessary process of reintegration, of carrying on in spite of fear, exhaustion, and the feelings of guilt and helplessness that I was now so far away from my loved ones, neighbours and the wider community.

Well, maybe — just maybe — this was my job. Talking intimately about what it was like for me, and perhaps them too, maybe even you. It was about putting a record down on paper, and leaving a trace; about finding a voice in the wake of an ongoing disaster that had destroyed so much physical heritage and *aides memoires*: our built environment, the history of human habitation in the shape of houses, churches and other historic buildings, the shapers of our material lives.

More and more it seemed to me that these structures were not only our external memory banks, they were also an internal geography, our shapes and roadmaps within. We would never be the same without them, but we could be healed if we saluted them and grieved for them. You will see I am not talking here about dead people but fallen buildings, the things we have made that can be rebuilt — while our loved ones are gone and can never be replaced.

That is true, but I think this is for a reason: memory is tied as equally to the place, the physical, as it is to the personal, the human. Te Taki Tairakena died with his students and many others in the CTV building collapse; while he is gone to what I believe is a better place, the site of that tragedy remains for us a wahi tapu, a sacred site — it is all we have here of his final moments. His remains rest now in the urupā of a Ngāti Haua marae near Morrinsville; for those of us left here, the place he departed this earth is as close as we can get to his old life, and his death.

We must rebuild and go on: the poetry is part of this renewal amidst the grief. Perhaps its presence can offer some answer to the questions of why and how we can go on making art, music, literature — all kinds of creative works — in the face of suffering and disaster. A poem in a sense is no different to a bus timetable: it tells us where and when we can continue our journey and go on to somewhere else. Poetry, said W. H. Auden, 'makes nothing happen', yet it is a happening in itself, it has a use value that cannot be quantified, yet may be enjoyed and inwardly experienced. A poem can happen within us. Poetry has kept me alive for many years now: when all else has failed, I can read and listen to that vital language 'in which man explores/his own amazement' — as Christopher Fry so crisply puts it.

Suffering? Again, Auden has something to say here, in his famous poem 'Musée des Beaux Arts', where he ruminates over Peter Brueghel the Elder's painting *Landscape with the Fall of Icarus*.[2] He announces his subject in the first two words, and the first two lines: 'About suffering, they were never wrong/the Old Masters …' In this ekphrastic poem (poetry based on a work of art), Auden meditates on the persistence of human suffering, and how art can capture but not prevent tragic events. In Brueghel's painting life goes on: the ploughman in the foreground ploughs, the ship in middle ground sails off with its cargo — perhaps like the container vessel *Rena* about to strike a hidden reef — while in the far background, almost unobserved, Icarus falls to his doom in the sea.

Using a few sharp images — 'the torturer's horse/ scratches its innocent behind on a tree' — he shows that while someone is enjoying life, or just making do, over the next hill or beyond the nearest ocean someone else will be getting the news of a terminal diagnosis, or lying trapped in a fallen building. Is this meant to be comforting? That depends on where you stand. It reminds me to take nothing for granted: the ploughman cannot help Icarus, not knowing of his plight. If he were to get the bad news from afar, for him to stop readying the earth for planting would be of no help to the dead flyer. Sometimes just carrying on is the best help of all: looking after the next person you meet on the road, the one closest to you.

When somebody died on the West Coast, where I grew up, neighbours and friends would always come with baking, with envelopes stuffed with money, with offers of help, a load of coal, the loan of a car, offers to mind the children, or just to sit with you making tea and small talk. They could not bring the dead one back, but they could take over some of life's burdens and tasks for the bereaved family. The earthquakes threw us all in Christchurch together — literally. Neighbours who had never, or hardly ever, spoken to each other began to behave like Blackball and Runanga mining people. They came, they gathered, they shared houses, food, water and care. They became more human as the tragedy and the losses enlarged them. Poetry is part of that sharing, and one that can nourish needs and hungers that food and drink are not intended to reach: our invisible selves.

Returning in May 2011 from a trip to Japan and the United States I was stuck in San Francisco for a day after mis-reading my departure time, arriving in the morning when the flight actually left in the evening. I had time on my hands, a good twelve hours. In one of the rest areas there is a magnificent 100-foot-long mural-cum-painting event, *Gateway*, the work of Ik-Joong Kang. It consists of 5265 oblong 3'×3' blocks, each with an image or symbol attached, and variations on a number of nouns attached to an unlikely adjective, such as Happy, or Tiny. Happy Pigment, Happy Separation, Happy Intimacy runs one theme; Tiny Spasm, Departed

Sister — the play on words with associated objects goes on and on. A flute, a clock, a plastic hamburger, a Madonna — the abstract tapestry of life in a blizzard of found objects. They somehow made their own reality, the kind of sense beyond the everyday daze we can so often bumble through on autopilot.

Kang had randomly assembled this panoramic grid of life's detritus, the size of the blocks determined by the size of his rucksack, as he travelled backwards and forwards to his studio on the Bay Area Rapid Transit trains. While I was marvelling at this feat of imagina-

Gateway, Ik-Joong Kang

tion, two women came and spent at least half an hour gazing at the montage, photographing and discussing with great animation this monument to life's bizarre riches. They were truly lost in that artwork: yet while they were so engrossed, all around them out of view, near and far, an Icarus no doubt was somewhere fall-

ing. Suicide bombers were making plans, earthquakes rattled the world, Vietnam vets and Iraq war survivors huddled half-crazed under freeway flyovers, and the pilot who would fly them to their destination was singing in the shower.

Should the existence of suffering preclude the pursuit of creative work? What if inevitable human pain and trouble can be mitigated and somehow healed by artistic effort and creativity? Poetry may not be able to answer that question, but at its very best poetry demands that we pay attention, just as the poet did in the making: attention to the richness, power and potential of language. A poem can send us back out into this troubled and marvellous world prepared to live more fully. There will surely continue to be all manner of suffering in this world, whether or not there is art or poetry — but without art, without poetry, such sufferings seem to me to be more meaningless and, worse, more powerful.

With poetry and all the other human arts we can tell our stories in such a way as to offer a measure of transcendence of suffering and a reacquaintance with delight. If, as Adorno famously opined, 'to write a poem after Auschwitz is barbaric', then art was no longer possible, the inhuman had defeated the human, the devils and the Nazis had truly won.[3] The Christchurch earthquakes have rewritten all our scripts: it would be a waste of their awesome forces to balk now at publishing those personal dictations Rūaumoko and Papatūānuku have inscribed so deeply on our collective life.

1 Cesar Vallejo, from 'Los Heraldos Negros/The Black Messengers', 1919; Clayton Eshleman's translation, *Poemas Humanos/Human Poems*, Cape, 1969
2 W. H. Auden, 'Musée des Beaux Arts', 1938
3 Theodor Adorno, from 'Cultural Criticism and Society', in *Prisms*, MIT Press, Cambridge, Mass., 1981

The end of the old Press building, Cathedral Square. *Press*